ARLINGTON NATIONAL CEMETERY
A Photographic Tour

PHOTOGRAPHS BY TARA BRUNDICK AND PATRICIA BRUNDICK

Aerial view, Arlington National Cemetery.

Eastern National provides quality educational products and services to the visitors to America's national parks and other public trusts.

Visit us at www.eParks.com.

The Donning Company Publishers
184 Business Park Drive, Suite 206
Virginia Beach, VA 23462

Library of Congress Cataloging-in-Publication Data

Arlington National Cemetery : a photographic tour.
   p. cm.
    ISBN 978-1-57864-450-6
1. Arlington National Cemetery (Arlington, Va.)—Pictorial works. 2. Soldiers' monuments—Virginia—Arlington—Pictorial works. 3. Sepulchral monuments—Virginia—Arlington—Pictorial works. 4. Arlington National Cemetery (Arlington, Va.)—Guidebooks.
   F234.A7A76 2008
   917.55'295—dc22

2007027605

Printed in the United States of America by Walsworth Publishing Company

Eastern National
Serving the Visitors to America's
National Parks and Other Public Trusts

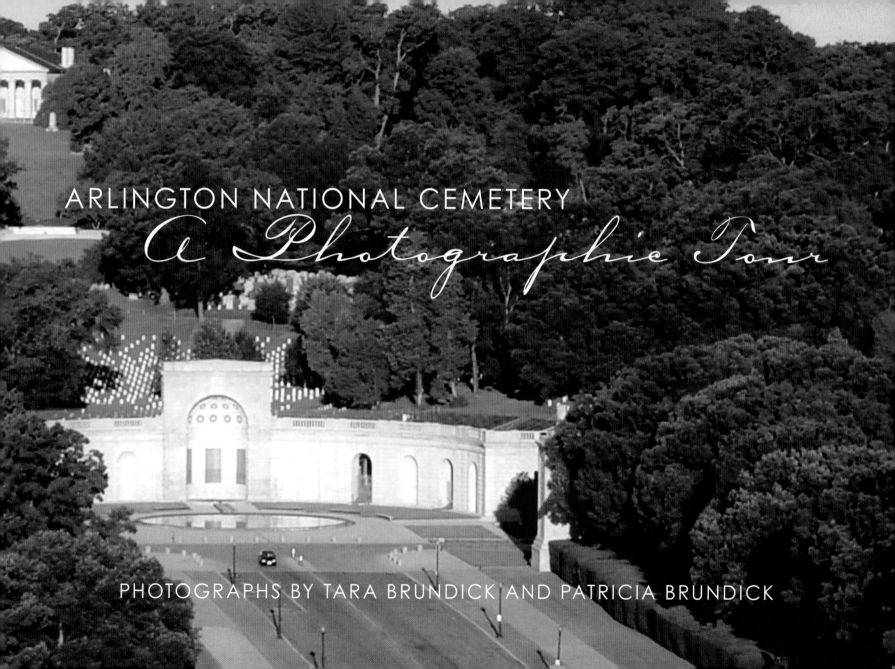

ARLINGTON NATIONAL CEMETERY
A Photographic Tour

PHOTOGRAPHS BY TARA BRUNDICK AND PATRICIA BRUNDICK

ARLINGTON NATIONAL CEMETERY:
A History

The land of Arlington National Cemetery has a rich history. George Washington Parke Custis, the adopted grandson of George Washington, chose the Virginia hillside overlooking Washington, D.C., as a living memorial to the great general and the first president of the United States. In 1857, Custis died and willed the property to his daughter, Mary Anna Randolph Custis, who had married Robert E. Lee in 1831. After they had lived more than thirty years at Arlington, the onset of the Civil War forced the Lees to leave their home. In May 1861, the Union army occupied the grounds and the mansion, converting them into an army camp and headquarters.

Two years later, a dispute over payment of property taxes cost the Lees their home, which was then sold to the U.S. government at a public auction. Later in 1863, the government used part of the estate to establish Freedmen's Village, a settlement for freed slaves. For more than thirty years, Freedmen's Village provided food, housing, education, medical care, and job training to the former slaves; thirty-eight hundred were buried in the cemetery. The village was closed in 1900.

In spring 1864, the Union army began burying its dead in the grounds of Arlington. The first burial was Private William Christman of Pennsylvania. In June of that year,

《 Gate to Arlington National Cemetery.

Quartermaster General Montgomery C. Meigs set aside two hundred acres of the estate for interments, and Arlington officially became a military cemetery.

The legal battle over the property continued after the war. Custis Lee, the general's oldest son, sued the federal government to regain the property. In 1882, the Supreme Court decided in his favor; but as there were sixteen thousand graves in the cemetery and Freedmen's Village was still operating, Custis took a cash settlement of $150,000, and the property remained in federal hands.

One of the most recognizable monuments in the cemetery is the Tomb of the Unknowns. The tomb holds the remains of a serviceman each from World War I, World War II, and the Korean War. Previously, the tomb held the remains of a serviceman killed in the Vietnam War, but he was later identified and removed at the request of his family.

The Tomb of the Unknowns is guarded twenty-four hours a day, 365 days a year. The Changing of the Guard ceremony takes place hourly from October through March and every half hour from April through September. While guarding the tomb, sentinels take twenty-one steps, face the tomb for twenty-one seconds, and repeat the process until the end of their tour. This is in homage to the highest military honor, the twenty-one-gun salute.

Another of Arlington National Cemetery's most visited sites is the grave of President John F. Kennedy. The grave includes the Eternal Flame, lit by his widow, Jacqueline Bouvier Kennedy, just days after his assassination. The former first lady is buried next to her husband, along with two of their children. Kennedy's brother, Senator Robert F. Kennedy, is also interred nearby; he was

⌄ *Arlington House, the Robert E. Lee Memorial.*

assassinated in 1968 while campaigning for president.

America's most decorated soldier, Audie Murphy, is one of many military heroes buried at Arlington. Throughout his service, Murphy earned twenty-eight medals; he went on to star in more than forty movies.

At his request, John J. Pershing, General of the Armies, was laid to rest atop a hillside surrounded by the graves of soldiers he commanded in World War I. The highest-ranking American general wanted no special marker, only a simple headstone amidst the men that served with him in "the war to end all wars."

Arlington National Cemetery Visitors Center. ⌃

General Daniel "Chappie" James, Jr., the military's highest-ranking African American officer in the Air Force, was buried at Arlington in 1978. The distinguished James flew seventy-eight combat missions during the Vietnam War.

Arlington National Cemetery is also the final resting place of many prominent civilians. Pierre Charles L'Enfant, the French architect who designed and planned Washington, D.C., was reinterred in 1909 to a site near Arlington House. William Howard Taft, the only American to serve as both the president of the United States and chief justice of the U.S. Supreme Court, was buried here in 1930. His wife, Helen Herron Taft, who played an integral role in bringing the Japanese cherry blossom trees to Washington, D.C.,

joined him in 1943. Their grave is marked by a fourteen-foot Stony Creek granite monument. Other U.S. Supreme Court justices buried at Arlington include Earl Warren, Thurgood Marshall, and William Rehnquist.

《 *McClellan Gate.*

Prominent space explorers are laid to rest in the cemetery, including Dick Scobee and Michael Smith, who died in the Challenger shuttle explosion in 1986. John Wesley Powell, the explorer of the Grand Canyon, is buried in Section One. Joe Louis, the former world heavyweight boxing champion who fought nearly one hundred exhibition matches to aid relief efforts in World War II, is buried near the Tomb of the Unknowns. Glenn Miller, the famous big band leader who went missing in action in December 1944, is commemorated with a memorial headstone.

Several recent monuments honor victims of terrorism. A pentagon-shaped memorial listing the names of the one hundred and eighty-four people killed in the September 11, 2001, attack on the Pentagon stands in Section 64; sixty-four of the victims are buried nearby. Twenty-one marines who were killed in the Beirut bombing of 1983 are laid to rest near Navy Seabee Robert Stetham, who was murdered during the TWA hijacking in 1985.

While the Department of Veterans Affairs administers most national cemeteries, the Department of the Army runs Arlington National Cemetery. The cemetery conducts approximately twenty to thirty funerals a day. Full honors funerals, whose origins date back to the Civil War, include a six-horse drawn caisson, a marching band, firing party, and a bugler to play "Taps." Interments exceeded three hundred thousand in 2005. Land adjacent to the cemetery has been transferred to the Army, which will allow the cemetery to stay active until approximately 2060.

Kennedy family gravesite and Eternal Flame
President John Fitzgerald Kennedy is buried here
along with his wife, Jacqueline Bouvier Kennedy
Onassis; his son, Patrick, who died in infancy; and
a daughter who was stillborn.

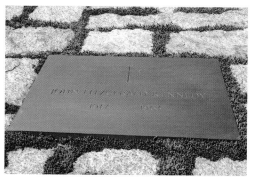

⌃ President John Fitzgerald Kennedy (top) and his wife, Jacqueline Bouvier Kennedy Onassis (bottom).

« Kennedy gravesite; Washington Monument in background.

⌃ Robert F. Kennedy, former Attorney General, Senator, presidential candidate, and brother of President John F. Kennedy, was shot on June 5, 1968, and died the next morning. Senator Robert Kennedy's funeral is the only one ever to take place at night at Arlington National Cemetery.

⌃ *Oliver Wendell Holmes—Civil War veteran, U.S. Supreme Court Justice, 1902–1932.*

General Daniel "Chappie" James, Jr., United States Air Force, was the first African American four-star General in the United States Armed Forces.

DANIEL "CHAPPIE" JAMES, JR.
GENERAL
UNITED STATES AIR FORCE
WORLD WAR II - KOREA - VIETNAM
FEB. 11, 1920 – FEB. 25, 1978
OUR BELOVED AND DEVOTED
WIFE, MOTHER AND GRANDMOTHER
DOROTHY WATKINS JAMES
JUNE 27, 1921 – MAY 2, 2000

《 Equestrian statue of Sir John Dill, British Field Marshal, World War II. His gravesite is marked with one of only two equestrian statues in the cemetery. Dill's gravesite is located in Special Section 32.

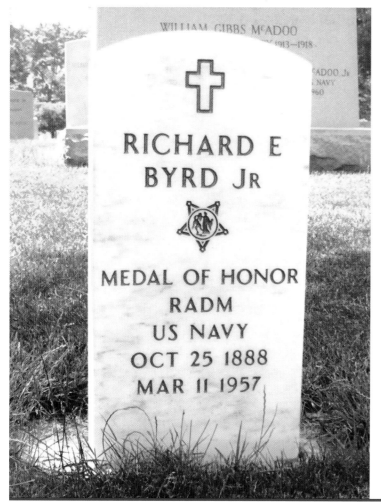

⌄ *Admiral Richard E. Byrd, Jr.—South Pole explorer.*

⌃ *Joe Louis (Barrow)—World heavyweight champion boxer and World War II veteran.*

Tomb of the Unknowns—1917–1918 (center tomb), 1950–1953 (left), 1957–1975 (center), 1941–1945 (right). The Tomb contains the remains of unknown American soldiers from World Wars I and II, the Korean Conflict and, until 1998, the Vietnam War. The Tomb is guarded 24 hours a day, 365 days a year by specially trained members of the Third United States Infantry, also known as The Old Guard.

HERE RESTS IN
HONORED GLORY
AN AMERICAN
SOLDIER
KNOWN BUT TO GOD

Tomb of the Unknowns. ⌃

Tomb of the Unknowns—
Changing of the Guard ceremony.

⌃ *Major Audie Murphy—One of the most decorated World War II soldiers and postwar actor.*

« *Spanish-American War Nurses Monument.*

>> (Left) Mast from the USS *Maine* (1898). (Opposite) Graves for sailors of the *Maine*. There are now 229 *Maine* casualties buried in Section 24 at Arlington beside the memorial. Of these, the identities of 62 are known, and the rest remain unknown.

HIGH FLIGHT

OH, I HAVE SLIPPED THE SURLY BONDS OF EARTH
AND DANCED THE SKIES ON LAUGHTER-SILVERED WINGS.
SUNWARD I'VE CLIMBED, AND JOINED THE TUMBLING MIRTH
OF SUN-SPLIT CLOUDS—AND DONE A HUNDRED THINGS
YOU HAVE NOT DREAMED OF—WHEELED AND SOARED AND SWUNG
HIGH IN THE SUNLIT SILENCE. HOV'RING THERE,
I'VE CHASED THE SHOUTING WIND ALONG, AND FLUNG
MY EAGER CRAFT THROUGH FOOTLESS HALLS OF AIR.
UP, UP THE LONG, DELIRIOUS, BURNING BLUE
I'VE TOPPED THE WINDSWEPT HEIGHTS WITH EASY GRACE
WHERE NEVER LARK, OR EVEN EAGLE FLEW.
AND WHILE WITH SILENT, LIFTING MIND I'VE TROD
THE HIGH UNTRESPASSED SANCTITY OF SPACE,
PUT OUT MY HAND, AND TOUCHED THE FACE OF GOD.

JOHN GILLESPIE MAGEE, JR.

⌃ *Back of Challenger Memorial—poem by John Gillespie Magee, Jr.*

⟨⟨ *Space Shuttle Challenger Memorial.*

❯ *Space Shuttle* Columbia Memorial.

IN MEMORY OF THE CREW OF
UNITED STATES SPACE SHUTTLE COLUMBIA
1 FEBRUARY 2003

IN HONOR OF MEMBERS OF THE
UNITED STATES ARMED FORCES WHO
DIED DURING AN ATTEMPT TO RESCUE
AMERICAN HOSTAGES HELD IN IRAN
25 APRIL 1980

★ U.S. MARINE CORPS ★

JOHN D. HARVEY   GEORGE N. HOLMES JR.
SGT   CPL
30 MAY 1958   20 JULY 1957

DEWEY L. JOHNSON
SSGT
26 MAY 1948

★ U.S. AIR FORCE ★

RICHARD L. BAKKE   HAROLD L. LEWIS JR.
MAJ   MAJ
13 MAY 1946   26 FEBRUARY 1945

JOEL C. MAYO
TSG
26 OCTOBER 1945

LYN D. McINTOSH   CHARLES T. McMILLAN
MAJ   CAPT
11 OCTOBER 1946   4 OCTOBER 1951

❮ *Iran Rescue Mission Monument.*

The Tomb of the Unknowns—Civil War Dead, was dedicated in 1866. It contains the remains of 2,111 unknown soldiers whose remains were gathered from the battlefields of Bull Run and the route to the Rappahannock.

BENEATH THIS STONE
REPOSE THE BONES OF TWO THOUSAND ONE HUNDRED AND ELEVEN UNKNOWN SOLDIERS
GATHERED AFTER THE WAR
FROM THE FIELDS OF BULL RUN, AND THE ROUTE TO THE RAPPAHANNOCK.
THEIR REMAINS COULD NOT BE IDENTIFIED, BUT THEIR NAMES AND DEATHS ARE
RECORDED IN THE ARCHIVES OF THEIR COUNTRY; AND ITS GRATEFUL CITIZENS
HONOR THEM AS OF THEIR NOBLE ARMY OF MARTYRS. MAY THEY REST IN PEACE!
SEPTEMBER, A.D. 1866.

Arlington House, the Robert E. Lee Memorial. ⌃

Pierre Charles L'Enfant, designer of the Capital City, reinterred at Arlington in 1909.

⌃ Gravesite of Chief Justice and President William Howard Taft.

« Confederate Monument—Memorial dedicated by the United Daughters of the Confederacy, located at Jackson Circle.

Confederate soldier headstones—
located at Jackson Circle.

⌃ Section 27—Nearly thirty-eight hundred "citizens" or "contrabands" (former slaves who were living in Freedmen's Village on the Arlington Estate) are interred in Section 27. "Citizen" or "civilian" is inscribed on their headstones. (Netherlands Carillon in the background is administered by the National Park Service and stands outside of Arlington National Cemetery.)

⌃ Newcomb Family Memorial.

≫ Dr. Anita Newcomb McGee was the first woman Army surgeon in 1898 and founder of the Army Nurse Corps in 1900.

≪ Iwo Jima Monument—U.S. Marine Corps War Memorial (stands outside Arlington National Cemetery, adjacent to the Ord and Weitzel Gate).

⌃ *John W. Weeks, Lieutenant, U.S. Navy, Secretary of War 1921–1925.*

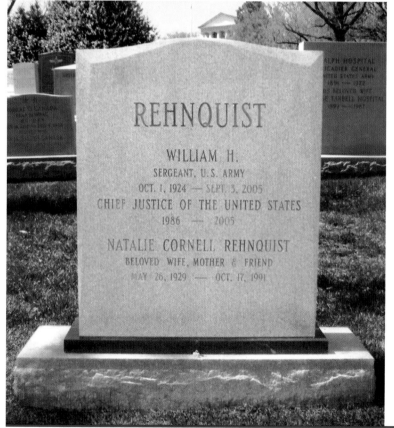

❯ *William H. Rehnquist—Sergeant, U.S. Army, Chief Justice, U.S. Supreme Court 1986–2005.*

REHNQUIST

WILLIAM H.
SERGEANT, U.S. ARMY
OCT. 1, 1924 — SEPT. 3, 2005
CHIEF JUSTICE OF THE UNITED STATES
1986 — 2005

NATALIE CORNELL REHNQUIST
BELOVED WIFE, MOTHER & FRIEND
MAY 26, 1929 — OCT. 17, 1991

CHIEF JUSTICE
WARREN EARL BURGER
SEPTEMBER 17, 1907 – JUNE 25, 1995

AND HIS BELOVED WIFE
ELVERA STROMBERG BURGER
OCTOBER 1, 1907 – MAY 30, 1994

❮ *Warren Earl Burger—Chief Justice, U.S. Supreme Court 1969–1986.*

THURGOOD MARSHALL
ASSOCIATE JUSTICE
1967 — 1991
UNITED STATES SUPREME COURT
JULY 2, 1908 — JANUARY 24, 1993

⌃ *Thurgood Marshall—first African American Associate Justice, U.S. Supreme Court.*

HARRY ANDREW BLACKMUN
NOVEMBER 12, 1908 – MARCH 4, 1999

Associate Justice
Supreme Court of the United States
1970 – 1994

His Wife
DOROTHY CLARK BLACKMUN
DECEMBER 12, 1910 – JULY 13, 2006

⌃ *Harry Andrew Blackmun—Associate Justice, U.S. Supreme Court.*

≫ *Major Elwood "Woody" Thomas Driver served as one of the original Tuskegee Airmen, an all-African American Army Air Corps combat unit of World War II.*

The Old Amphitheater was dedicated in 1874. For many years, it was home to the annual Memorial Day observances as well as to other special meetings and observances.

Major General Philip Kearny (Civil War) equestrian statue and grave—one of only two people honored with an equestrian statue and grave in Arlington National Cemetery.

⌃ *Pan Am Flight 103 Memorial Cairn. On December 21, 1988, Pan Am Flight 103 exploded over Lockerbie, Scotland. This act of terrorism killed all 259 people on board as well as 11 on the ground.*

The Memorial Amphitheater (inset and opposite) was dedicated on May 15, 1920. Many ceremonies are conducted here, including the annual Veterans Day Service, a Memorial Day Service, and a Sunrise Easter Service.

Easter Sunrise Service at Arlington Cemetery Memorial Amphitheater.

⌃ *Annual Memorial Day Service at amphitheater.*

THE BEGINNING OF THE END OF WAR LIES IN REMEMBRANCE
HERMAN WOUK

IN SACRED MEMORY OF THOSE AMERICANS WHO GAVE THEIR
LIVES DURING THE KOREAN WAR, 1950-1953

54,246 DIED   8,177 MISSING IN ACTION   389 UNACCOUNTED FOR POW

FIRST INTERNATIONAL TRIBUTE,   JULY 27, 1987
GIVEN BY   NO GREATER LOVE   AND THE   KOREAN WAR VETERANS ASSOCIATION

⌃ The Korean War Contemplative Bench was dedicated July 27, 1987. It is located on the north side of the Memorial Amphitheater beside the Korean White Pine tree donated by President Kim of Korea in 1965.

In 1925, Canadian Prime Minister Mackenzie King proposed a memorial to the large number of United States citizens who enlisted in the Canadian Armed Forces and lost their lives during World War I. Because the Canadians entered the war long before the United States, many Americans enlisted in Canada to join the fighting in Europe. On Armistice Day 1927, the monument was dedicated. Designed by Canadian architect Sir Reginald Bloomfield, the monument consists of a bronze sword adorning a 24-foot gray granite cross.

⌃ *Third Infantry Division, U.S. Army.*

Memorial to the soldiers and sailors of Spanish-American War.

∧ The Battle of the Bulge Memorial is dedicated to the over nineteen thousand casualties of this campaign fought on the western front during World War II.

≪ The Rough Riders was the nickname of the First U.S. Voluntary Cavalry, which distinguished itself in combat in Cuba during the Spanish-American War. The most famous member of the unit was Theodore Roosevelt, who as president dedicated this memorial in 1906.

IN MEMORY OF OUR MEN IN FRANCE
1917 — 1918

⌃ *John Foster Dulles—U.S. Army Major, Secretary of State.*

《 The remains of many servicemen buried in Europe during World War I were disinterred, then either reinterred in selected cemeteries in Europe or returned to the United States. Of these, the remains of about 2,100 were reinterred in Arlington National Cemetery, specifically in Section 18. Through the efforts of the Argonne Unit American Women's Legion, the Argonne Cross was erected to their memory and in their honor.

Monument to Jane Delano and all military nurses who died during World War I—Stands watch over the nurses section of Arlington National Cemetery. Delano was the second superintendent of the U.S. Army Nurse Corps.

⋁ Earl Warren— Governor of California, Chief Justice of U.S. Supreme Court 1953–1969.

EARL WARREN
GOVERNOR OF CALIFORNIA
CHIEF JUSTICE OF THE UNITED STATES
1953 —— 1969

"WHERE THERE IS INJUSTICE, WE SHOULD CORRECT IT; WHERE THERE IS POVERTY, WE SHOULD ELIMINATE IT; WHERE THERE IS CORRUPTION, WE SHOULD STAMP IT OUT; WHERE THERE IS VIOLENCE WE SHOULD PUNISH IT; WHERE THERE IS NEGLECT, WE SHOULD PROVIDE CARE; WHERE THERE IS WAR, WE SHOULD RESTORE PEACE; AND WHEREVER CORRECTIONS ARE ACHIEVED WE SHOULD ADD THEM PERMANENTLY TO OUR STOREHOUSE OF TREASURES."
1972

Civil War Union soldiers' headstones.

⌃ General James H. Doolittle—U.S. Air Force.

⌃ Actor Lee Marvin—Private First Class, U.S. Marine Corps,
   World War II.

⌃ Colonel Stuart Allen Roosa—U.S. Air Force,
   Apollo 14 Command Module pilot.

OMAR NELSON BRADLEY
GENERAL OF THE ARMY
1893 — 1981
LOVING WIFE
ESTHER DORA BRADLEY
1922 — 2004

MARY QUAYLE BRADLEY
1892 — 1965

⌄ *Chaplains from four wars rest on Chaplains Hill in Section 2.*

⌃ *Omar Bradley—General of the Army.*

⌃ U.S. Coast Guard Memorial.

» Robert E. Peary—Arctic explorer, credited for many years as discoverer of the North Pole.

ROBERT EDWIN PEARY
DISCOVERER OF NORTH POLE
APRIL 6, 1909

« Matthew Henson—Co-discoverer of the North Pole with Robert E. Peary. Henson, the first African American to reach the pole, planted the U.S. flag.

⌄ In 1980, the first Columbarium Complex was opened at Arlington, consisting of nine buildings for the inurnment of cremated remains. As of 2008, there are over forty-seven thousand remains located in these buildings.

The U.S. Air Force Memorial overlooking Arlington National Cemetery.

THE PENTAGON   SEPTEMBER 11 2001

MICHAEL A NOETH DM2 USN
♦ BARBARA K OLSON
♦ RUBEN S ORNEDO
DIANA B PADRO
JONAS M PANIK LT USN
CLIFFORD L PATTERSON JR MAJ USA
♦ ROBERT PENNINGER
♦ ROBERT R PLOGER III & ZANDRA F PLOGER
DARIN H PONTELL LT USN
SCOTT POWELL
JACK D PUNCHES CAPT USN RET
JOSEPH J PYCIOR JR AW1 USN
♦ LISA J RAINES
DEBORAH A RAMSAUR
★ RHONDA SUE RASMUSSEN
MARSHA D RATCHFORD IT1 USN
MARTHA M RESZKE
♦ TODD H REUBEN
CECELIA E (LAWSON) RICHARD
EDWARD V ROWENHORST
JUDY ROWLETT
ROBERT E RUSSELL SGM USA RET
WILLIAM R RUTH CW4 USA
CHARLES E SABIN SR
MARJORIE C SALAMONE
♦ JOHN P SAMMARTINO
DAVID M SCALES COL USA
ROBERT A SCHLEGEL CDR USN
JANICE M SCOTT
MICHAEL L SELVES LTC USA RET
MARIAN H SERVA
DAN F SHANOWER CDR USN
ANTIONETTE M SHERMAN
DONALD D SIMMONS
♦ GEORGE W SIMMONS & DIANE M SIMMONS
CHERYLE D SINCOCK

GREGG H SMALLWOOD ITC USN
GARY F SMITH LTC USA RET
♦ MARI-RAE SOPPER
♦ ROBERT SPEISMAN
PATRICIA J STATZ
EDNA L STEPHENS
♦ NORMA LANG STEUERLE
LARRY L STRICKLAND SGM USA
♦ HILDA E TAYLOR
KIP P TAYLOR LTC USA
♦ LEONARD E TAYLOR
SANDRA C TAYLOR
♦ SANDRA D TEAGUE
KARL W TEEPE LTC USA, RET
TAMARA C THURMAN SGT USA
OTIS V TOLBERT LCDR USN
WILLIE Q TROY SSG USA RET
RONALD J VAUK LCDR USN
KAREN J WAGNER LTC USA
META L (FULLER) WALLER
CHIN SUN PAK WELLS SPC USA
MAUDLYN A WHITE SSG USA
SANDRA L WHITE
ERNEST M WILLCHER
DAVID L WILLIAMS LCDR USN
DWAYNE WILLIAMS MAJ USA
MARVIN ROGER WOODS RMC USN RET
♦ JOHN D YAMNICKY SR CAPT USN RET
♦ VICKI YANCEY
KEVIN W YOKUM IT2 USN
DONALD M YOUNG ITC USN
EDMOND G YOUNG JR
LISA L YOUNG
♦ YUGUANG ZHENG & SHUYIN YANG CHINA
★ = NO IDENTIFIED REMAINS
♦ = AMERICAN AIRLINES FLIGHT 77

⌃ *Arlington National Cemetery.*

《 *Memorial to the 184 people who died at the Pentagon on September 11, 2001.*

Arlington National Cemetery.

≪ *U.S. Army firing party.*

≪ *U.S. Navy pallbearers.*

U.S. Marine Corps Band.

⌃ U.S. Air Force.

≪ U.S. Navy.

≪ U.S. Marine Corps bugler.

⩔ U.S. Air Force.

U.S. Coast Guard.

President John F. Kennedy—Section 12

Senator and Attorney General Robert F. Kennedy—Section 45

Oliver Wendell Holmes, Civil War veteran and Supreme Court justice—Section 5

Equestrian statue of Sir John Dill, British field marshal, WWII—Section 32

Daniel "Chappie" James, Jr., first African American four-star general, USAF—Section 2

Richard E. Byrd Jr., admiral and polar explorer, Medal of Honor recipient—Section 2

Joe Louis (Barrow), world heavyweight champion boxer, WWII veteran— Section 7A

Tomb of the Unknowns—Adjacent to Memorial Drive

Nurses Memorial, Spanish-American War to the present—Section 21

Audie Murphy, one of the most decorated WWII soldiers—Section 46

Mast of USS *Maine*, sunk in Havana Harbor— Section 24

Memorial to the crew of the Space Shuttle *Challenger/Columbia*—Section 46

Iran Rescue Mission Memorial for the servicemen killed in hostage rescue attempt—Section 46

Tomb of the Unknown Civil War Dead, remains of 2,111 Union soldiers—Section 26

Arlington House, restored memorial to Confederate General Robert E. Lee— Adjacent to Sherman Drive

Pierre Charles L'Enfant, designer of the capital city, reinterred here in 1909— Section 2

William Howard Taft, president and chief justice—Section 30

Confederate Monument, marking a section for the burial of Confederate soldiers—Section 16

Dedicated to the U.S. Colored Troops and residents of Freedmen's Village (and Netherlands Carillon)—Section 27

Iwo Jima, United States Marine Corps Memorial—Outside Arlington National Cemetery, adjacent to Ord & Weitzel Gate

Anita Newcomb McGee, organizer of Army Nurse Corps— Section 1

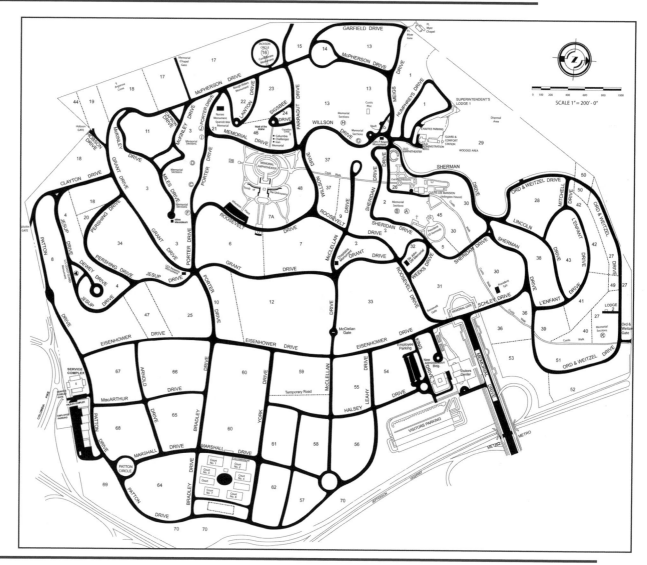

Additional Sites

(Seen upon entering Arlington National Cemetery)
Arlington National Cemetery Visitor Center
Memorial Gate Entrance
McClellan Gate

(Near Kennedy gravesite and Sir John Dill)
Lieutenant John W. Weeks, Secretary of War
William H. Rehnquist
Warren Earl Burger
Thurgood Marshall
Harry A. Blackmun
Elwood "Woody" Thomas Driver (Tuskegee Airman)

(Near Arlington House)
Old Amphitheater
Major General Philip Kearny (Civil War general)
Pan Am Flight 103 Memorial Cairn

(Near Tomb of the Unknowns and space
    shuttle memorials)
Memorial Amphitheater
Korean War Contemplative Bench
Canadian Cross of Sacrifice Memorial
Third Infantry Division Monument
Spanish-American War Memorial

(Near Confederate Soldiers Monument)
Rough Riders Memorial
Battle of the Bulge Memorial
Argonne Cross (WWI)
Nurses Memorial

John Foster Dulles
Chief Justice Earl Warren

(Near Section 27 Freedmen's Village)
Civil War Union soldiers' headstones
William Christman (first military serviceman
    interred at Arlington)

(Near Joe Louis Barrow)
James H. Doolittle
Lee Marvin
General of the Army Omar Bradley
Colonel Stuart Allen Roosa
Chaplains Hill Monument

(On Jessup Drive)
Coast Guard Memorial
Admiral Robert Edwin Peary
Matthew Henson

(East side of cemetery)
Columbarium
September 11, 2001, Attack on the
    Pentagon Memorial

(South end of cemetery, outside gates)
U.S. Air Force Memorial